C000184821

the way of the cross

Rob Frost

National Distributors

UK: (and countries not listed below)
CWR, Waverley Abbey House, Waverley Lane, Farnham, Surrey GU9 8EP.
Tel: (01252) 784700 Outside UK +44 1252 784700

AUSTRALIA: CMC Australasia, PO Box 519, Belmont, Victoria 3216.
Tel: (03) 5241 3288

CANADA: Cook Communications Ministries, PO Box 98, 55 Woodslee Avenue, Paris, Ontario.
Tel: 1800 263 2664

GHANA: Challenge Enterprises of Ghana, PO Box 5723, Accra.
Tel: (021) 222437/223249 Fax: (021) 226227

HONG KONG: Cross Communications Ltd, 1/F, 562A Nathan Road, Kowloon.
Tel: 2780 1188 Fax: 2770 6229

INDIA: Crystal Communications, 10-3-18/4/1, East Marredpalli, Secunderabad – 500026, Andhra Pradesh.
Tel/Fax: (040) 27737145

KENYA: Keswick Books and Gifts Ltd, PO Box 10242, Nairobi.
Tel: (02) 331692/226047 Fax: (02) 728557

MALAYSIA: Salvation Book Centre (M) Sdn Bhd, 23 Jalan SS 2/64, 47300 Petaling Jaya, Selangor.
Tel: (03) 78766411/78766797 Fax: (03) 78757066/78756360

NEW ZEALAND: CMC Australasia, PO Box 36015, Lower Hutt.
Tel: 0800 449 408 Fax: 0800 449 049

NIGERIA: FBFM, Helen Baugh House, 96 St Finbarr's College Road, Akoka, Lagos.
Tel: (01) 7747429/4700218/825775/827264

PHILIPPINES: OMF Literature Inc, 776 Boni Avenue, Mandaluyong City.
Tel: (02) 531 2183 Fax: (02) 531 1960

SINGAPORE: Armour Publishing Pte Ltd, Block 203A Henderson Road, 11–06 Henderson Industrial Park,
Singapore 159546.
Tel: 6 276 9976 Fax: 6 276 7564

SOUTH AFRICA: Struik Christian Books, 80 MacKenzie Street, PO Box 1144, Cape Town 8000.
Tel: (021) 462 4360 Fax: (021) 461 3612

SRI LANKA: Christombu Books, 27 Hospital Street, Colombo 1.
Tel: (01) 433142/328909

TANZANIA: CLC Christian Book Centre, PO Box 1384, Mkwepu Street, Dar es Salaam.
Tel/Fax (022) 2119439

USA: Cook Communications Ministries, PO Box 98, 55 Woodslee Avenue, Paris, Ontario, Canada.
Tel: 1800 263 2664

ZIMBABWE: Word of Life Books (Pvt) Ltd, Christian Media Centre, 8 Aberdeen Road, Avondale,
PO Box A480 Avondale, Harare, Zimbabwe, Tel: (04) 333355 or 091301188

For email addresses, visit the CWR website: www.cwr.org.uk
CWR is a registered charity – Number 294387
CWR is a limited company registered in England – Registration Number 1990308

Copyright © 2005 CWR

Published 2005 by CWR, Waverley Abbey House, Waverley Lane, Farnham, Surrey GU9 8EP, England.

The right of Rob Frost to be identified as the author of this work has been asserted by him in accordance with the Copyright, Designs and Patents Act 1988, sections 77 and 78.

All rights reserved. No part of this publication may be reproduced, stored in a retrieval system, or transmitted, in any form or by any means, electronic, mechanical, photocopying, recording or otherwise, without the prior permission in writing of CWR.

Unless otherwise indicated, all Scripture references are from the Holy Bible: New International Version (NIV), copyright © 1973, 1978, 1984 by the International Bible Society.

Front cover image: Design Pics Inc.
Concept development, editing, design and production by CWR
Printed in Slovenia by Tiskarna Ljubljana

ISBN 1-85345-353-6

Contents

Contents

Introduction

During the 40 days of Lent some people give up chocolate or try to fast on a Friday. This devotional guide sets an even more demanding agenda.

It aims to change your view of the world; to help you discover what it means to follow the 'way of the cross'; to set a personal agenda of preparation for the most sacred event in the Christian calendar.

This study can be used by groups during the days of Lent, or as the focus for homegroups at any time of the year. Above all, this guide seeks to establish the way of the cross as integral to the life and spirituality of every contemporary Christian.

How to use this study guide – a note for the group leader

The chemistry of each group is different, and an experienced leader will quickly discover the kind of 'level' at which most members of the group are happy to operate.

The aim of each study is to provide enough options for the leaders to mix a blend of discussion, study and comment suitable for their group.

Some groups will be much happier relating personal experiences, telling stories and sharing in a conversational level. Select the more 'human questions' and sections for them.

Other groups will enjoy delving into the Old Testament, comparing and contrasting the 'way of the cross' as seen in prophecy and in the life of Jesus, and exploring the other biblical 'windows' into the theme. There is ample material for this kind of fellowship to explore!

And some groups, perhaps not used to discussion or study, may prefer to linger over the devotional elements. They should feel free to spend longer on the readings, read comments and prayers and to limit discussion to basic questions about the passages.

There are too many discussion questions for any one group meeting. It would be helpful if the leader could select questions particularly relevant to the level of the group.

Whatever kind of group you are in, my prayer is that this material will bring you closer to each other and closer to walking the 'way of the cross'.

Devotional Sections

I once preached at two churches. One was very traditional, and the service consisted of a harvest festival, a christening, the dedication of new Sunday school teachers, my 'guest' sermon and the usual liturgy of hymns, prayers and Bible readings. We were catapulted into a huge agenda of 'religious activity' until my head was spinning! I dunked my biscuit in a lukewarm cup of tea after the benediction and wondered what the whole exercise had been about!

A few weeks later I was preaching at a much more 'Pentecostal' style of service. There was over an hour of mega-decibel music from a vast worship band. The congregation hopped and danced, and I was nearly decapitated by several large ladies with flags which were waved incessantly over the congregation throughout the proceedings! I munched my jam-filled doughnut and sipped the strong coffee afterwards, hoping that soon my nerves might stop jangling!

On neither occasion did I sense 'the beyond', that sense of 'otherness', that experience of transcendence ... which is at the heart of true Christian spirituality. On neither occasion did I genuinely feel that I was in the Presence of the Living God. I was never 'lost in wonder, love and praise'.

My hope is that you will give space for the devotional sections to be rich and meaningful at the start and close of each meeting. They are designed to support the meaning and the message of each meeting.

The opening and closing devotional content should be seen as material to get you started, rather than the final article! My hope is that you will give plenty of time for meditation, prayer, listening to music and even for silence.

The Early Church Fathers
In each of the studies I have quoted from the Early Church Fathers in the devotional section. They were the church leaders who instructed the Church in the teaching of the apostles during its early days of development. The Fathers are often identified as the church leaders active before the Council of Chalcedon in 451. They wrote against a background of great doctrinal conflict, and they didn't always agree with each other! In this postmodern age, in which everyone is searching for 'roots', I believe that the writings of these brilliant theologians have much to say to us. The contemporary Church has much to learn from them at a time when biblical truth is increasingly under scrutiny. I hope that the excerpts included here will encourage you to explore more of this rich devotional treasure!

The Structure
There are ten sections to each study. Don't feel that you have to use all ten for your group, and don't feel that you have to stick rigidly to the order in which they're set out! Each group is very different, and personally I often 'jump about' in the running order according to how the flow of conversation in the group is going.

My work with developing new styles of group work over the last three years and observing different groups in process has lead me to ask the fundamental question 'what makes a group really successful'?

Three aspects have really impacted me during this research for a study series called 'Essence'.

1. Buzz Factor! Groups can descend into a real 'low' once they get going. There is a buzz of conversation before the group starts and after it finishes, but people often 'clam up' during the group itself. My research revealed that people felt the group worked best when the buzz of conversation ran throughout, and people were 'alive' and 'engaged'. So that's why there are discussion questions throughout! The evening should be seen as an ongoing conversation rather than 'leader sections' and 'group sections'. People enjoy talking about their lives, their experiences and their 'week', and rather than discouraging this we should actively encourage it – though constantly relating these experiences to the theme with questions like 'so what does that experience teach you about … servanthood?' etc.

2. Trust Factor! People get far more out of a group if they have really experienced 'agape' fellowship'. An important aspect of this is the building up of trust among the group, and this comes by laughter, the sharing of personal experiences and expression of personal need. Some groups despise the 'Conversation Starter' activities, feeling that they are demeaning! My experience, however, is that when you spend time getting to know each other, laughing together and talking on a more superficial level at first … that trust grows and people are more willing to reveal their true feelings later on.

3. Group Leadership! I like leading groups, and I probably like the sound of my own voice! My observation of the process of groups, however, is that this can build a kind of hierarchy in the group. Groups seem to work much better if there is a greater group ownership of the whole evening's programme. Instead of just the leader doing the sections such as 'Bible Echoes' or 'Insights', get others to prepare them and share them, so that you as the leader are free to facilitate and oil the wheels of participation rather than focusing on your next piece of input. People in the group will learn far more if they have prepared things to share than by sitting listening to you! (We leaders find this hard!)

The Sections

Conversation Starters: Please make sure that you have prepared the 'props' beforehand. Involve others in bringing things, too, so that they feel ownership. If this activity really 'takes off' don't despair, laughter and sharing here can pay dividends later!

Prayer Time: I have generally tried to encourage corporate prayer here. You might like to brief two or three folk to pray, even reading out a prayer they prepared earlier. If we can model 'open prayer' here it will encourage others who have never prayed out loud to do so. *Do* make it clear, however, that there's no compulsion to speak prayers if people don't want to. Silence can be golden!

Focus: This just guides the group into the general area for the study. Feel free to dump this and either tell a personal story or get someone in the group with a relevant testimony or experience to share it if you want to!

Bible Reading: I've used the NIV or Today's NIV, sometimes you might like to read the passage from two different versions. Why not get a member of the group to prepare the reading beforehand, so that it's read well?

Bible Echoes: This section will be of special interest to groups who enjoy in-depth Bible study. For such groups you may care to make this section the focus for the whole evening. Track through the comparison passages and get people to dig deep into the Old Testament. I found the material here fascinating, and there's enough in each of these sections for a full evening in itself!

Insights: I've generally used things which I found fascinating, with a high interest factor! You may like to go back to the passage again and look at it in the light of what is here.

Observations: This is the bulk of my exposition. I hope people won't just read it, but make it their own in some way! If you are the group leader deliver this as if you discovered these things for yourself, personalise the content and make it live!

Talk Time: As previously stated, groups can sometimes reach a 'dead end' here. When they're ordered to 'discuss' there can be a kind of 'group silence' which is a form of protest against the leader! This is much less likely to happen if the group have been chatting all along. Remember basic groups skills about not allowing one person to dominate, keep giving new opportunities for others to take part. Always thank people for their contributions and be kind (even when you disagree!)

Response: As an evangelist I'm always looking for and expecting a response! Too many groups conclude the evening with no response and everyone goes home 'having had a nice time'. For me a group only really works if there is a challenge for a response and an opportunity to respond to the Word. This is one part of the evening I wouldn't give away. As the leader I would want to put the challenge of the Word and evoke some kind of personal response!

Closing Devotions: Please don't hurry these. People need to learn how to be quiet, how to reflect, to meditate and to pray. I have deliberately steered these closing devotions to be more reflective. After all the laughter, chatter and sharing during the evening this is the time when we focus on Jesus and draw the strength and grace we need to fulfil this particular challenge in the way of the cross!

the way of *intimacy*

Key Character: Mary, the sister of Martha
Keynote Symbol: The oil
Key Challenge: To develop a closer walk with Jesus

Conversation Starter

Pass around some adverts for perfume from magazines.

What do the images used by the advertising copywriters say about each perfume?

Anyone who has ever been out shopping for perfume will know what it's like to use a 'tester!' Pass around the group four different kinds of perfume, asking everyone to spray a little on their hand. (Make sure that no one in the group is allergic to this kind of substance!) No one speaks until all four brands have been used. (Members of the group might like to note down a score out of ten for each brand, and write what they like or dislike about it.) Play some classical music as this is done (eg a short section from the Brahms *Requiem*).

- What do you like and dislike about each brand and why?
- What is your favourite kind of natural flower scent?
  Does it bring back memories of somewhere specific?

Prayer Time

Thank God for the gift of smell. Each person should try to remember some lovely natural scent or fragrance (like honeysuckle or freshly mown grass) and thank God (silently, or out loud) for the beautiful places they remind us of.

Focus

We live in a world of accelerating speeds of communication. In any given day we might receive messages by email, voice-mail, text message or letter. Wherever we go we might be contacted via a mobile phone, by broadband hyperlink, through a palm-pilot, laptop or pager.

Travel on a train today and you're likely to be surrounded by people having conversations on the phone but who never speak to the passenger beside them. Communication seems to increase as intimacy declines!

With so many distractions, it's little wonder that many of us struggle with the most important form of communication of all – prayer and meditation.

We might find it easier to communicate with Jesus by email, for email doesn't demand as much of us as prayer! If we are to discover an intimate level of relationship with Him it demands a deep level of spiritual and emotional engagement. This takes time and practice.

The way of the cross is a journey towards an ever-closer relationship with Jesus Christ. It's a journey towards intimacy.

- What makes a good friendship?
- Do you consider Jesus as your friend?
- What kind of friend is Jesus?

Bible Reading

John 12
Jesus Anointed at Bethany

Six days before the Passover, Jesus arrived at Bethany, where Lazarus lived, whom Jesus had raised from the dead. Here a dinner was given in Jesus' honour. Martha served, while Lazarus was among those reclining at the table with him. Then Mary took about a pint of pure nard, an expensive perfume; she poured it on Jesus' feet and wiped his feet with her hair. And the house was filled with the fragrance of the perfume.

But one of his disciples, Judas Iscariot, who was later to betray him, objected, 'Why wasn't this perfume sold

and the money given to the poor? It was worth a year's wages.' He did not say this because he cared about the poor but because he was a thief; as keeper of the money bag, he used to help himself to what was put into it.

'Leave her alone,' Jesus replied. 'It was intended that she should save this perfume for the day of my burial. You will always have the poor among you, but you will not always have me.'

Meanwhile a large crowd of Jews found out that Jesus was there and came, not only because of him but also to see Lazarus, whom he had raised from the dead. So the chief priests made plans to kill Lazarus as well, for on account of him many of the Jews were going over to Jesus and putting their faith in him.

- What can you remember of the story of the 'raising of Lazarus'?
- What kind of dinner party do you think this was meant to be?
- Why do you think Mary chose this moment to anoint Jesus?
- What does this incident tell us about Judas?
- What does it tell us about Mary?
- Can you remember what happened on any other occasions when Jesus was anointed like this?

Bible Echoes

The Jews used scent and fragrance in their ceremonies from the earliest times. Even in the book of Exodus we read how Aaron took a censer filled with incense and burning coals from the altar and hurried into the centre of the assembly of people to 'make atonement for them'.

The plague had already started among the people, but Aaron offered the incense and made atonement for them. He stood between the living and the dead, and the plague stopped. (Num. 16:47–48)

Incense was used with the grain offering (Lev. 2:1f) and it was offered with the shwbread (Lev. 24:7–9). Incense was made from stacte, onycha, galbanum and frankincense. No other ingredients were permitted (Exod. 30:9; 34–35). Frankincense is a resinous gum and bitter to taste. Its name comes from the 'freeness' with which it burns – giving off a steady flame for a long time. It was particularly used to sweeten the smell at times of sacrifice and it was traditionally seen as the symbol of deity. Of course, frankincense was one of the gifts given to the baby Jesus in Bethlehem. The fact that Mary anointed Jesus with a strong-smelling ointment was reminiscent of the sweet smell associated with sacrifice.

- In Protestant churches we rarely use incense. Have we lost some symbolism because of this?
- Do you think we should use scent in worship and liturgy?
- What could it symbolise for us today?

Insights

The woman who anointed Jesus used 'a pound of costly perfume of pure nard' (John 12:3). The word 'pure' can also mean 'faithful' or 'genuine' and may be hinting at the kind of quality of Mary's love for Jesus.

Nard is an oil which comes from the root of the nard plant. It's a perennial herb, often used as a medicinal ointment and it was generally imported from Nepal and India. That was why it was so expensive! A 'pound' was a very generous quantity for Mary to use, so it's little wonder that it caused a reaction among some of the disciples and that the 'whole house was filled with fragrance'!

It's interesting that Mary anointed Jesus' feet. It would have been much more customary to have anointed His head with such an expensive perfume. Often, however, the anointing of a body for burial began with the feet rather than the head.

When Mary undid her hair to wipe the feet of Jesus it was quite an unusual thing to do. Jewish women kept their hair tied up, and would only let it loose when undressing for a husband or as a sign that they were in mourning. She would probably have had her hair loose when mourning for Lazarus (John 11:32), and now she looses it again.

The combination of anointing, pouring the nard on His feet and loosening her hair all indicate that Mary was thinking about the death of Jesus as she expressed her love for Him so powerfully. This was an act of complete abandon. Of unreserved love. A sign of the intimate friendship she shared with her Lord.

- What is 'intimacy with God'?
- How can we discover it for ourselves?
- Can we experience this corporately as well as individually?

Observations

There are a number of different accounts of Jesus being anointed. In one of them, in Luke 10, we read that there was some tension between Mary and her sister Martha. While Mary was intently listening to Jesus, Martha was busy in the kitchen! Eventually Martha came to Jesus and asked him to order her sister into the kitchen to help!

'Martha, Martha,' the Lord answered, 'you are worried and upset about many things, but only one thing is needed. Mary has chosen what is better, and it will not be taken away from her.' (vv.41–42)

Mary had discovered the importance of a deep and loving relationship with Jesus. This spirituality is what lies at the centre of true Christianity, the roots of which go back deep into Old Testament history. It seems ridiculous that so many people are turning to the latest 'Californian Guru' when they could discover a spirituality which has stood the test of time.

Way back in the twelfth century the great Christian theologian, Richard of St Victor, wrote, 'The third degree of love is when the mind of man is ravished into the abyss of divine light, so that the soul, have forgotten all outward things.'

There are hundreds of Christian mystics like Richard, whose writings down the centuries have enriched and refreshed the Church and which could introduce a new generation to this 'third degree of love'.

In a busy and stressful world, many are desperate to know how to discover inner peace, and how to meditate and reflect. It's little wonder that our 'busy' and 'noisy' church services can be such a turn off! There is often little or no space to 'practise the presence of God' in these agenda-driven and noisy celebrations. Those groups who are daring to move beyond the familiar format of the five-hymn sandwich or the worship-song medley are discovering what a blessing it can be when we create space to glimpse the glory of God! We live in a world desperate for intimacy and hungry for spirituality. The question is – how can we in the Church model a richness of Christian spirituality which will engage with this need?

Talk Time

1. What kind of personality differences do you think were there between Mary and Martha?

2. Jesus implies that Mary has actually made a choice (see Luke 10). What had she chosen – and what were the implications of her choice?

3. Does 'intimacy with Jesus' begin with a choice? If so, what are you choosing?

4. Christian mystics sometimes describe their devotional discipline as 'practising the presence of God'. What do you think they mean by that?

5. What does the story of Mary say to the thousands of people today who are exploring 'New Age spirituality'?

6. Is our Christian devotion too confined to buildings?

_____

_____

_____

_____

7. The Ten Commandments remind us to rest on the 'Sabbath'. What is this rest and why is it important?

_____

_____

_____

_____

8. Have we lost something with the arrival of Sunday trading – if so, what?

_____

_____

_____

_____

9. How can we develop a meaningful discipline of Sabbath observance which will enhance our relationship with Jesus?

_____

_____

_____

_____

10. How can we encourage our Sunday worship to become a richer experience spiritually?

_____

_____

_____

Response

For many of us, our devotional life has become a series of hasty 'arrow prayers', a short reading from Bible notes, or a sing-along 'praise tape' while we drive. Sunday has become a long list of 'to do' jobs which build up during a hectic week. Our devotional life is fed by occasional conventions or praise and worship celebrations.

Intimacy with Jesus Christ begins with a commitment to cultivate the presence of the living God throughout the minutes and hours of every waking day. Prayer doesn't need to be a formal lengthy exercise that we only get round to occasionally, but an everyday offering of all of our activities to God.

So everyday activities like driving the car, attending a business meeting, shopping in the supermarket or travelling on a train should be seen as something to be offered to God – and those we meet along the way as being people to serve and to pray for. In this way the whole of life becomes worship. Every moment carries the possibility of new intimacy with Jesus Christ.

- Why did the women go to the tomb early that first Easter morning? What was motivating them (see Luke 24)?
- How could they best show their love now that Christ was risen?
- How best can we show our love for Jesus today?

Closing Devotions

You may wish to use scented candles or even a stick of 'incense' during this closing devotional period. It is a reminder of the fragrance of sacrifice and the power of Mary's love offering. We will use one of the prayers of Saint Augustine. You may like to read it in sections, with pauses, over a piece of orchestral music.

Late have I loved thee, O beauty so ancient and so new; late have I loved thee: for behold thou wert within me, and I outside; and I sought thee outside and in my unloveliness fell upon those lovely things that thou hast made.

Thou wert with me, and I was not with thee. I was kept from thee by those things, yet had they not been in thee, they would not have been at all.

Thou didst call and cry to me to break open my deafness: and thou didst send forth thy beams and shine upon me and chase away my blindness: thou didst breathe fragrance upon me, and I drew in my breath and do now pant for thee: I tasted thee, and now hunger and thirst for thee: thou didst touch me, and I have burned for thy peace.

- Have you ever been through a time which mystics describe as 'the dark night of the soul', when Jesus seemed far away?
- How did you move beyond that experience?
- Does our relationship with Jesus change with the years? If so, how?

the way of service

Key Character: Peter
Keynote Symbol: A towel
Key Challenge: To develop a life of care for others

Conversation Starter

Provide neutral shoe polish and shoe-cloths for each person in the group. Then each cleans the shoes of at least one other person in the group! Keep the shoes with you for the next activity!

- What would be the contemporary equivalent of washing someone's feet? Discuss.

Prayer Time

Origen was one of the earliest Christian theologians. He was born in Africa (probably Alexandria) towards the end of the second century. He endured terrible torture during the Decian persecution in about AD 250. This is one of his prayers:

> O Jesus, my feet are dirty. Come even as a slave to me, pour water into your bowl, come and wash my feet. In asking such a thing I know I am overbold but I dread what was threatened when you said to us, 'If I do not wash your feet I have no fellowship with you.' Wash my feet then, because I long for your companionship.

Either silently or out loud pray for the person whose shoes you are holding. Pray that God will bless that person and help him or her to discover the love of Jesus and to walk 'the way of service'.

Focus

The starting point of the road which is the 'way of the cross' is not in becoming 'like a servant', but in allowing Jesus to become the servant who 'washes' us.

When Jesus offered to wash Peter's feet His disciple was appalled. 'Lord ... you... wash ... my ... feet' (John 13:6)? But Peter had to learn that allowing Jesus to serve us is the hallmark of full and total surrender. And until we have been served by Him we cannot possibly know how to serve the world.

● Why do some people find it hard to be 'served' by Jesus?

Bible Reading

John 13

Jesus Washes His Disciples' Feet

It was just before the Passover Feast. Jesus knew that the time had come for him to leave this world and go to the Father. Having loved his own who were in the world, he now showed them the full extent of his love.

The evening meal was being served, and the devil had already prompted Judas Iscariot, son of Simon, to betray Jesus. Jesus knew that the Father had put all things under his power, and that he had come from God and was returning to God; so he got up from the meal, took off his outer clothing, and wrapped a towel around his waist. After that, he poured water into a basin and began to wash his disciples' feet, drying them with the towel that was wrapped round him.

He came to Simon Peter, who said to him, 'Lord, are you going to wash my feet?'

Jesus replied, 'You do not realise now what I am doing, but later you will understand.'

'No,' said Peter, 'you shall never wash my feet.'

Jesus answered, 'Unless I wash you, you have no part with me.'

'Then, Lord,' Simon Peter replied, 'not just my feet but my hands and my head as well!'

Bible Echoes

'When he had gone a little farther, he saw James son of Zebedee and his brother John in a boat, preparing their nets' (Mark 1:19).

'Simon Peter, Thomas (called Didymus), Nathanael from Cana in Galilee, the sons of Zebedee, and two other disciples were together' (John 21:2).

- Read and compare these two stories involving James and John.
- What did serving Christ mean on the first occasion?
- What did it mean on the second?
- What did it actually mean to these disciples to live a life of service?

Insights

Servants and slaves were a common part of Roman middle-class life. A visit to any Roman archaeological site like Ephesus reveals a society based on an 'upstairs downstairs' view of life. A society of masters and servants!

The dusty dirty roads of Palestine led to dirty and dusty feet! Open-toed sandals were the common footwear, and sometimes feet were caked in mud and grime. When people arrived it was customary to provide water to wash them with, and in better-off homes a servant would be provided to do it for you! Historians tell us that such tasks were not allocated to Jewish male servants – they would only be given to women, children or Gentiles.

On special occasions foot-washing was a sign of great love and respect for a superior. So a disciple might occasionally wash the feet of his rabbi or a wife might wash her husband's feet. But in Jesus' case the roles are reversed. Jesus does for us what we are not prepared to do for each other.

- At a wedding reception would you prefer to be sitting at the top table or 'waiting on' the guests? Why?
- Do you find it harder to give or to receive?

Observations

A symbol for the 'way of the cross' is a towel. Jesus made it clear that it wasn't good enough just to have time for others but to be 'sensitive to the touch of the needy' – as He was to the woman with a haemorrhage when He was hurrying to heal a sick child.

For Jesus, it wasn't good enough to talk about feeding the hungry, He took a boy's packed lunch of bread and fish to feed an enormous crowd. He didn't just talk about forgiveness but embraced those whose lives were broken and messed up. He didn't just talk about wholeness but made the Gerasene demoniac whole. He didn't just talk about caring but washed His disciples' feet. He didn't just talk about love but hung on a cross to demonstrate the breadth of it.

He chose a path of total service, a path that would often exhaust and drain Him. A path which made enormous personal demands along every step of the way. If we are to follow Jesus on the 'way of service' we must put God on the throne and ourselves at His service. When we engage in God-centred living, we are not doing something special: we are only fulfilling what He expects of us.

Of course, this style of Christian living is costly, yet it opens us up to being in the centre of the Lord's will. When we allow each day to be fully His, we ourselves

become fully His. At last we can honestly say to the Lord that we are wholly available.

There are some teachers you never forget. When I was a teenager, one of my college lecturers was a tall bearded man with an unapproachable manner. He was always reciting his favourite motto: 'You have all of my sympathy, but none of my time.' He lived by what he said: it was hard to talk to him because he was always rushing off somewhere. I didn't want his sympathy, whereas I often needed a few moments of his time. But he was always too busy.

I'm sure many of us have so filled our lives with 'important' activities that we are not available to respond to God-opportunities for service. Day after day we rush from one place to the next, offering everyone we meet 'all of our sympathy but none of our time'.

Some of us are moving through life at such a speed that we meet people but don't get to know them. We hear people but don't listen to them. We look at people but don't see their need. We miss opportunities for serving those around us. We say to the Lord, 'Anytime, but not just now!' The Lord sends people into our life for many reasons but, sadly, we sometimes regard them as 'interruptions' to our busy schedule. In doing so, we are missing out on wonderful opportunities for witness. We have not discovered the joy and excitement of walking the 'way of service'.

- Name ten incidents in which Jesus served others.
- What did the life of service cost Him day by day?
- Describe the manner in which Jesus served people.
- What kind of attitude did He demonstrate?

Talk Time

1. What kind of tasks do you think servants and slaves carried out in a Roman villa?

   _____

   _____

   _____

2. What kind of contemporary jobs would you ask a 'servant' to do for you if you had one?! (Finding a parking space? Setting the video-recorder?)

   _____

   _____

   _____

3. If Jesus lived in your area whom would He serve first?

   _____

   _____

   _____

   _____

4. What are the rewards of Christian service?

   _____

   _____

   _____

   _____

5. Do you ever feel you're not appreciated, or treated like a doormat?

   _____

   _____

   _____

   _____

6. If you are in genuine Christian 'service' should you expect to be appreciated?

_____

_____

_____

7. What marks out a person as 'truly great'?

_____

_____

_____

Response

The way of the cross is about entrusting ourselves to Jesus. If you're an activist you might find it much easier to 'do' rather than to 'wait'. The way of service begins, however, when we allow Jesus to wash our feet. To serve us. To love us. To cleanse us. To befriend us. There are many in the Church who have not yet humbled themselves, admitted their need and allowed the servant-like love of Jesus to reach them, to transform them and to melt their proud hearts.

But the way of the cross is also about following His example, and about living a life for others rather than ourselves. This is distinctly counter-cultural. For in a society focused on 'me' it isn't easy to live a life focused on 'them'.

Many of us feel caught up in the strong current of self-preoccupation which is prevalent in society today. We must recognise, however, that whenever we make the choice to do something selfless, sacrificial or servant-like, we will discover the lasting joy of 'the way of service'.

Some years ago I had chicken pox very badly. After ten days in bed I was very weak and could barely walk. The doorbell rang, and there was an 82-year-old lady from the women's fellowship at a nearby church. On a bitterly cold day she had taken two buses and walked to my home. She presented me with a bottle of 'tonic', whispered a simple but profound prayer, kissed me on the cheek and left.

It was an utterly selfless act. In my days of weakness it touched me at a level I couldn't describe. I've often thought of it. Sometimes the towel of service can mean doing something so simple, yet something so profound.

- What would living a life of service actually mean?
- How would our lives change if we all took this seriously?
- How would the world change?

Closing Devotions

The group session could end with a demonstration of a foot-washing, with two previously invited participants taking part! Play a piece of music or a worship song such as 'Servant King' while this is being done. As the music continues, one person washes the other's feet – and then the positions are reversed.

(As this happens pass a towel very slowly around the group. Each person is invited to think about and pray for the people whom they are called to serve.)

- Ask the two participants in the foot-washing to explain how it felt.
- You might like as a group to share names or situations where you are called to serve. Some may like to receive prayer for 'grace' to serve these people or those in these situations.

We read a song at the end of the devotional time which suggests that we should learn how to serve Christ in the shadow of God's guiding hand. It is a traditional Methodist hymn, sung at ordination services when people offer themselves for life-long service in the church. It reminds us that the love we need for service comes from God Himself.

Captain of Israel's host and Guide
Of all who seek the land above,
Beneath thy shadow we abide,
The cloud of thy protecting love;
Our strength, thy grace; our rule, thy word;
Our end, the glory of the Lord.

By thine unerring Spirit led,
We shall not in the desert stray;
We shall not full direction need,
Nor miss our providential way;
As far from danger as from fear,
While love, almighty love, is near.

Charles Wesley

SCENE THREE

the way of suffering

Key Character: James and John
Keynote Symbol: A cup
Key Challenge: To walk the path of suffering

Conversation Starter

The good old days: Try and remember something which
happened a long time ago (eg for the over 60s, the
Coronation)! Try to describe what you can remember of it!
To this day, traditional Jews celebrate the Passover meal
and recite the great events of the Passover night to the
young children who are present.

- What happened on Passover night? As a group piece
  together all that you can remember about the slavery in
  Egypt, the plagues, Pharaoh and the Red Sea crossing.

Prayer Time

Our prayer is a traditional anthem of African-Americans.
It looks back across the journey they have travelled with
thanksgiving, and asks for God's continued help and
guidance.

> God of our weary years,
> God of our silent tears,
> Thou who hast brought us thus far on the way;
> Thou who hast by thy might led us into the light;
> Keep us for ever in the path, we pray.
> Lest our feet stray from the places, our God, where we
>   met Thee;
> Lest, our hearts drunk with the wine of the world, we
>   forget thee,
> Shadowed beneath thy hand,
> May we for ever stand ...

During a piece of music, look back over your life, and
think about times when things were particularly difficult.
Remember how the Lord and other people helped you
through those difficult days and give thanks to God for
them. Some of the group may like to give thanks out loud.

Focus

In the world there is often a queue of people to fill roles that are high profile and important. Sometimes there's not such a rush to do the washing-up or to sweep the floor!

In Luke's account of the Last Supper the meal is followed by a squabble between the disciples about who will be the greatest in the kingdom. This is reminiscent of the incident described in Mark 10 in which James and John asked Jesus if He would allow one of them to sit at His right, and the other at His left in His new kingdom. Jesus answered their request (Mark 10:38): 'You don't know what you are asking. Can you drink the cup I drink or be baptised with the baptism I am baptised with?' James and John assured Him that they could drink of this cup and Jesus warned them: 'You will drink the cup I drink and be baptised with the baptism I am baptised with.'

Jesus was reminding them that there are greater priorities in His kingdom than being in positions of power! Sometimes we are called to suffer for the gospel, or to suffer with those who suffer and weep with those who weep.

- What was the cup and the baptism to which Jesus was referring?
- What did He say about this cup in the Garden of Gethsemane?
- How might we be called to suffer for the gospel, too?

Bible Reading

Luke 22:7-20

The Passover Meal

When the hour came, Jesus and his apostles reclined at the table. And he said to them, 'I have eagerly desired to

eat this Passover with you before I suffer. For I tell you, I will not eat it again until it finds fulfilment in the kingdom of God.'

After taking the cup, he gave thanks and said, 'Take this and divide it among you. For I tell you I will not drink again of the fruit of the vine until the kingdom of God comes.'

And he took bread, gave thanks and broke it, and gave it to them, saying, 'This is my body given for you; do this in remembrance of me.'

In the same way, after the supper he took the cup, saying, 'This cup is the new covenant in my blood, which is poured out for you.' (vv.14–20)

- What did Jesus mean by the words He spoke when He passed the disciples the cup?
- Do you think they understood the significance of them?
- What is the symbolism of the cup to us in the Holy Communion? When we drink from this cup what are we doing?

Bible Echoes

In the five 'servant songs' of Isaiah we find some beautiful and profound prophecies describing what God's promised 'messenger' would be like. Many scholars believe that these prophecies were fulfilled in the life and ministry of Jesus, and that His whole ministry can be summed up as that of a 'suffering servant'.

None of Isaiah's prophecies is more relevant to this than that found in Isaiah 53 – words quoted by Jesus in the synagogue at Capernaum at the very start of His own ministry. In identifying Himself with this 'servant', Jesus recognised that His ministry would be one intimately bound up with suffering.

Philip the evangelist also saw clearly that Isaiah was referring to Jesus in his beautiful prophecy. In Acts 8:26–39 the Ethiopian eunuch was reading Isaiah 53 when Philip joined him in his chariot. The eunuch asked, '... who is the prophet talking about, himself, or someone else?' And Luke tells us that 'Philip opened his mouth and beginning from this Scripture he preached Jesus to him" (Acts 8:35, NASB).

In all the history of Israel, no one comes close to fulfilling this prophecy besides Jesus. Jesus Himself said, 'The Son of man did not come to be served, but to serve [that is, to be the suffering servant] and to give his life a ransom [a substitute!] for many' (Mark 10:45). He defined His whole ministry in terms of suffering and sacrifice.

If we are to understand who Jesus was and why He came we cannot avoid seeing Him as 'God's *Suffering* Servant'. He came to save us, and did not buckle under the grief of carrying our rejection, for He bore our griefs.

He did not wither under the weight of our huge sorrows but carried them for us. He did not come to bring judgment on us but was pierced for us, dying in our place. He did not come to crush us but to be crushed for us. He took the punishment that should have been ours upon Himself in order that we might have peace and be healed.

Isaiah 53 reminds us that Jesus is the Servant who has borne our griefs and sorrows, who has been pierced for our transgressions, and crushed for our iniquities.

This is the 'suffering servant', whose suffering inspires us – but, more than that, whose suffering saves us and transforms us.

- In which ways do you see Jesus as a 'suffering servant'?
- How can He help us when we pass through times of suffering?

Insights

At the Last Supper scholars believe that Jesus was lifting the third cup of the Passover when He spoke the poignant words: 'This cup is the new covenant in my blood which is poured out for you.'

This third Passover cup was used after the participants had eaten the Passover lamb, the unleavened bread and the bitter herbs. It followed the explanation of why the meal was being celebrated, of how the lintels and doorposts of the Jewish slaves in Egypt were daubed in lamb's blood so that the plague might 'pass over' their homes, and how they had their bags packed in readiness for their exodus.

Although Jesus' words mirror earlier salvation events, He now puts the new symbolism of His own life and ministry into the use of the cup. His blood is the new sacrifice that will lead to their salvation. Whenever we drink from the cup at the Holy Communion we remember His suffering and sacrificial death for us, and drink deep of the 'cup of suffering'.

- Describe incidents in the ministry of Jesus in which He identified with the suffering – or was willing to suffer Himself ...

Observations

James and John clearly had misdirected ambitions in Christ's kingdom. They didn't seem to grasp what true greatness was really about.

Their story is a fascinating one; Jesus strode along the beach one day and invited them to leave their nets and become 'fishers of men'. He welcomed them to share the most intimate moments of His ministry and to watch and listen while He was healing and teaching. They witnessed the Transfiguration and they were there at the Last Supper and accompanied Him to the Garden of Gethsemane.

When James and John asked if they could sit beside Jesus 'in the kingdom' they had very ambitious plans (Mark 10:35–37). They wanted to be at the 'top table'! If one was to sit 'at His right', and the other 'at His left' they were hoping that they might take up the positions of prime minister and chancellor – with Jesus as the President! Their concept of greatness was built around ideas of political power and the false expectation that Jesus had come on earth to set up some kind of political state. Jesus made it clear that greatness in His kingdom was derived from a very different set of values. For Him, part of true greatness was a willingness to drink of the 'cup of suffering'.

In His ministry Jesus sought out people who suffered, like the leper, the madman, the prostitute and the tax-collector. He got alongside them; empathised with them; brought healing and comfort to them.

From borrowed stable to borrowed grave Jesus walked the path of those who suffer. His life was a life incarnate in suffering and immersed in rejection and pain. He was born a refugee, He was tempted in every way as we are, He was rejected – even by the people of His own town of

Nazareth, He was betrayed by one of His closest friends, and judged unfairly by the prejudices of His enemies.

He chose to walk a path of suffering. He walked the 'way of the cross' from the earliest days of His life until His dying breath that He might understand our suffering and share it with us. He invites us to walk that road too, and to drink deep of that cup of suffering, for this is the way of the cross. When we drink of this cup we are willing to suffer for Him, and to seek out those who suffer that we might love and comfort them.

Talk Time

1. Who is 'suffering' in your local area and community? How can you discover who they are, where they live and what they need?

   _____
   _____
   _____

2. How can you become Christ-like in your care for them?

   _____
   _____
   _____

3. Have you ever 'suffered' for the gospel?

   _____
   _____
   _____

4. You could read out testimonies from magazines published by agencies such as Christian Solidarity Worldwide or Release International. Or show a DVD from one of the agencies which support the persecuted church. What kind of suffering have these people known?

_____
_____
_____

5. What would the 'cup of suffering' mean to them?

_____
_____
_____

6. What would you be willing to die for?

_____
_____
_____

Response

James had an ambition to be 'great in the kingdom'. He discovered that true greatness is not about personal ambition and success but about following the way of the cross and the way of suffering.

I find it very powerful that James, one of the two brothers who had such a distorted view of the 'power structure' of God's kingdom, was an early Christian martyr. Historians believe that he was martyred for his faith in AD 44, during the time of the persecution by King Agrippa. We read about it in Acts 12:2 in the simple statement, '[Herod] had James, the brother of John, put to death with the sword.'

For James, the way of the cross was a way of suffering. For some Christians this 'way' may mean the ultimate sacrifice of offering our very lives. But for all of us it must involve a sacrifice of time, of effort, of caring, of serving and of loving.

The way of the cross is about living our lives as a daily celebration of the Saviour who drank the cup of suffering to fulfil the purposes of His heavenly Father. It's about seeking out those who are suffering, to weep with them and to share their pain. It's about being willing to lay our lives down for Him.

Read again Acts 12:2: the martyrdom of James by Herod.

- What kind of leader do you think James became?
- What events changed him most?
- Would you still go to church if it were against the law?
- Are you willing to suffer for the gospel?

Closing Devotions

Gregory was born in Cappadocia in about AD 330. He was brought up in a Christian home and at first it seemed that he was seriously considering becoming a priest. He was completely 'won over' by the rising tide of paganism, however, and married and became a teacher of rhetoric.

It was much later, under the influence of Basil, who became bishop of Caesarea, that Gregory found faith. His classical education and his new-found faith equipped him to become one of the greatest theologians and church leaders of his day. This 'Father' of the Church, Gregory of Nyssa, made the connection between the Incarnation and the atonement. We will use some of his words as a meditation to help us to understand why Jesus chose the path of suffering.

(These could be read over music.)

> Christ did not suffer death because He had been born;
> it was because of death that He chose to be born.
> Eternal Life had no need of life,
> but He entered our bodily existence in order to restore us from death to life.
> Our entire nature had to be recalled from death;
> Hence He stretched forth His hand, as it were, to the dead body, and came to see the place where we had fallen.
> Indeed He came so close to death as to touch mortality itself, that He might make of our own nature, in His body, a principle of resurrection.
> Amen

(As the music continues you may like to pass a large cup of wine from person to person and each think what the 'cup of suffering' might mean for you. Close with a time of prayer for those who suffer and for the persecuted church.)

the way of surrender

Key Character: Peter
Keynote Symbol: A yoke
Key Challenge: To offer everything to Christ

Conversation Starter

What was the longest night of your life?
The night ... Before an exam?
  Before an operation?
  Waiting for a teenager to come home?
  Giving birth to your first baby?
  The night after a big argument?
  Before you got married?
  Christmas Eve with excited kids?
  Some other traumatic experience?
What was it like?
Did you do anything to help pass the time?

Prayer Time

Thomas A. Dorsey was born near Atlanta in Georgia
in 1899. He started out his music career in a small jazz
band in Chicago, but later went on to dedicate his life to
writing gospel songs. This song, which is a cry to God
for guidance, was Martin Luther King's favourite hymn. It
might be particularly helpful during a long dark night!

Take my hand, Precious Lord,
Lead me on, let me stand.
I am tired, I am weak, I am worn.
Through the storm, through the night, lead me on to
  the light.
Take my hand, Precious Lord, lead me home.

When my way grows drear, Precious Lord, linger near
When my life is almost gone.
Hear my cry, hear my call, hold my hand, lest I fall.
Take my hand, Precious Lord, lead me home.

When the darkness appears and the night draws near
And the day is past and gone,

At the river I stand,
Guide my feet, hold my hand.
Take my hand, Precious Lord, lead me home.

Pray for people you know who are enduring 'long nights'
of hardship or difficulty at this time.

Focus

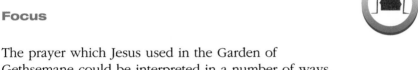

The prayer which Jesus used in the Garden of
Gethsemane could be interpreted in a number of ways.
When He said 'not my will, but yours be done' you could
read it as a prayer of defeat. (Huh … I've got no chance.)
Or you could see it as a prayer of resignation. (Whatever
will be, will be.) It could be muttered as a prayer of
inevitability. (There's no point in struggling, God is too
big to argue with!)

- Is there another way of reading this great prayer? How
  do you view it?
- Could you pray this prayer yourself?

Bible Reading

Matthew 26:36–46
Gethsemane

Then Jesus went with his disciples to a place called
Gethsemane, and he said to them, 'Sit here while I
go over there and pray.' He took Peter and the two
sons of Zebedee along with him, and he began to be
sorrowful and troubled. Then he said to them, 'My soul is
overwhelmed with sorrow to the point of death. Stay here
and keep watch with me.'

Going a little farther, he fell with his face to the ground
and prayed, 'My Father, if it is possible, may this cup be

taken from me. Yet not as I will, but as you will.'

Then he returned to his disciples and found them sleeping. 'Could you men not keep watch with me for one hour?' he asked Peter. 'Watch and pray so that you will not fall into temptation. The spirit is willing, but the body is weak.'

He went away a second time and prayed, 'My Father, if it is not possible for this cup to be taken away unless I drink it, may your will be done.'

When he came back, he again found them sleeping, because their eyes were heavy. So he left them and went away once more and prayed the third time, saying the same thing.

Then he returned to the disciples and said to them, 'Are you still sleeping and resting? Look, the hour is near, and the Son of Man is betrayed into the hands of sinners. Rise, let us go! Here comes my betrayer!'

- Why did Jesus so want the disciples to pray?
- Why was Jesus kneeling?
- What indications are there of how He was feeling?
- Compare how Jesus acted when the mob arrived to how the disciples behaved. (See later verses.) What do you think made the difference between how Jesus reacted and how they faced up to things?

Bible Echoes

Our plans and God's plans! Read together: Genesis 22; James 4:7–10, 13–15.

- What do both of these passages say about what we want and what God wants?
- Have you ever struggled with God's will for your life?
- Is sacrifice an integral part of obedience?
- Do you plan for the future?
- How should we plan?

Insights

The Garden of Gethsemane was believed by some
(Zech. 14) to be the place where the Messiah would
return as judge, so it is interesting that this is the location
for Christ's lonely struggle with the implications of the
next phase of His mission. The scene there is reminiscent
of the way in which Jesus was tested in the wilderness
over those 40 days. He is alone, He is at prayer, and He
is ministered to by an angel.

His anguish in the Garden was so great that some
scholars interpret the passage here as meaning 'it could
kill Him'. We can be sure that the devil was active in
many ways here, as he was in the wilderness.

At this point the will of God and the wishes of Satan
converge. Satan wants Jesus to drink of the cup of suffering
because he believes that it will be the means of His
destruction. God wants it, because He knows that through
this suffering Satan's power will be destroyed for ever.

The three disciples had just eaten a big meal, but it was
customary for guests at the Passover to sit and discuss
its meaning for several hours afterwards! Some Jewish
traditions taught that if the guests fell asleep before the
ceremonial meal was complete, they 'dissolved' the group
of which they were a part. So these disciples really had
no excuse to go to sleep!

It's sobering to realise that the three disciples mentioned
here were also present when Jesus was transfigured on
another mountain (see Matt. 17:1), and that one of them
had made a great display of his faithfulness (Matt. 26:35).
Even though they had a deep insight into Jesus' true
identity they were, even now, disobedient. Jesus had
really warned His disciples to pray, but they disobeyed
and preferred to sleep!

When we love God, we sometimes have to face things which we really don't want to go through. Loving God involves a choice to obey, no matter what the consequences. At last, when the long night is over, and the torches of His captors grow closer as they move up the hillside, Jesus calls His disciples to *rise* to face it – ready or not (26:45).

On many levels this incident is a powerful challenge to us all.

- How was Jesus tested in the wilderness?
- How is He tested here?
- What do you think He was asking God for in His prayers?
- Why were the disciples asleep?
- How do you think they felt when the mob arrived? What might they be facing?

Observations

Once, many years ago, I visited the tiny island of Sark, which is a short boat ride from Guernsey. No cars are permitted on the island, but near the jetty where the ferry pulls in there is a 'taxi rank' of horses and carts. Most of the 'round the island tours' were beyond my price range, but at the very end of the line was an elderly driver with an even more elderly looking 'old nag'. He offered to 'do a deal'!

The old man beamed at me with his one tooth, and explained that he'd only left Sark once – and that was for a day trip to Guernsey! The family and I climbed aboard the rickety old cart for a grand tour of the island. The horse clip-clopped ahead of us and the cart rattled and shook as we drove along the dusty track.

As the tour progressed, the driver handed the reins over to my very young son. I was worried. The boy hardly knew left from right, and as we drove past the cliff-tops I wondered if we might roll over! But when my son pulled right we turned right, and when he pulled left we turned left. The blinkered horse had no idea where he was headed; he simply obeyed. He trusted the driver implicitly.

Jesus said, 'Take my yoke and put it on you, and learn from me, because I am gentle and humble in spirit; and you will find rest. For the yoke I will give you is easy and the load I will put on you is light' (Matt. 11:29–30, GNB).

To be yoked to Christ means what it says. We are blinkered and He steers. We don't know the road ahead but He does. We are servants and He is Master. As we actively seek His guidance for our lives, we discover what it really means to be disciples.

We can't expect to plan our own lives in the Lord's service, nor choose the opportunities we think are best. We must actively seek the Lord's will and submit to it – even when we don't agree!

- How do you think it feels to wear a yoke?
- Why did Jesus describe His yoke as 'light?'
- How does God really guide us?

Talk Time

1. Why did Jesus struggle so much with that prayer in the Garden of Gethsemane?

   _____

   _____

   _____

2. Have you ever struggled with obedience to Christ, or in a decision that was painful as a Christian?

   _____

   _____

   _____

3. Is it always painful to be obedient to God?

   _____

   _____

   _____

4. What does it mean to 'lose your life for His sake'?

   _____

   _____

   _____

5. Sometime Christians are seen as the most miserable people on earth, but if we're obedient shouldn't we be the happiest people on earth?

   _____

   _____

   _____

Response

If we are to really walk the way of surrender we must become wholly submitted to Christ's will and purposes for our lives.

Anyone who has visited the church in Gethsemane cannot fail to have been moved by the huge rock around which it's built; a rock similar to the one where Jesus prayed His prayer of complete and utter submission to His Father's will. 'Father,' He said, 'if you will take this cup of suffering away from me. Not my will, however, but your will be done …'

It was a prayer prayed with great anguish of spirit, for He prayed it as sweat like great drops of blood fell from His face.

Obedience to God's will can sometimes involve huge personal sacrifice and great self-denial. Yet it's as we are willing to 'lose our life for His sake' that we find it.

- Why do you think that Jesus took James and John with Him to Gethsemane?
- If James and John had truly grasped the message about servant-hood, what would they have done for Jesus in the Garden of Gethsemane?

Closing Devotions

In the spring of 387, at the age of 33, Augustine went to Milan for the 40 days of preparation for baptism that preceded Easter. His journey to faith had been long, and at times tortuous, but at the Easter vigil service on the night of Holy Saturday Augustine was baptised by Ambrose. Many people at that time, when Christianity was the fashionable road to success in the Christian empire,

may have taken such a step casually and then returned to their old ways, but Augustine was not one of them.

> Grant me, even me, my dearest Lord, to know thee, and love thee, and rejoice in thee. And if I cannot do these perfectly in this life, let me at least advance to higher degrees every day, till I can come to do them in perfection.
> Let the knowledge of thee increase in me here, that it may be full hereafter. Let the love of thee grow every day more and more here, that it may be perfect hereafter; that my joy may be great in itself, and full in thee.
> I know, O God, that thou art a God of truth. Oh, make good thy gracious promises to me, that my joy may be full. Amen.
>
> Saint Augustine

- What does it actually mean to live a life of 'obedience to God'?
- Why does God always know best?

the way of **salvation**

Key Character: Adam
Keynote Symbol: A cross
Key Challenge: To know the saving power of Jesus Christ

Conversation Starter

One of the most popular subjects for films, books or plays is the battle between good and evil. Some of the greatest blockbuster movies of our generation have shown battle scenes involving countless creatures locked in mortal combat. Generally, good wins!

As an icebreaker, four people in the group should mime the titles of films, books or plays which have contained such scenes of the cosmic forces at war! The rest of the group should guess the title.

- Which is your favourite depiction of this theme?
- Why do you think so many pieces of contemporary art, film or drama feature this cosmic theme?
- Do any of these remind you of the Christian story?

Prayer Time

Dear Lord Jesus,
Thank You for walking the way of the cross for me.
Thanks for bearing the brokenness, suffering the pain and facing the rejection.
Thanks for taking into Yourself all that suffering.
Thanks for taking on Yourself all that sin.
Thanks for taking upon Yourself that battle with evil.
That we might discover...
    a new life to live
    a new strength in suffering
    a new forgiveness for sin
    a new power over evil
    a new hope for tomorrow
    Amen.

Thank God (either openly or silently) for those tough times when He has strengthened you and supported you.

Focus

The message of Easter reminds us that Christ's death on the cross was the Kairos moment in which human beings could discover deliverance. It was the moment of liberation from the power of death, evil and judgment. If we are to walk the way of the cross we can only do so in the power of Christ demonstrated through the cross and the resurrection. This is how we join the 'victory side' in the greatest cosmic battle of all time.

Bible Reading

John 12:20-33

Jesus Predicts His Death

Now there were some Greeks among those who went up to worship at the Feast. They came to Philip, who was from Bethsaida in Galilee, with a request. 'Sir,' they said, 'we would like to see Jesus.' Philip went to tell Andrew; Andrew and Philip in turn told Jesus.

Jesus replied, 'The hour has come for the Son of Man to be glorified. I tell you the truth, unless a grain of wheat falls to the ground and dies, it remains only a single seed. But if it dies, it produces many seeds. The man who loves his life will lose it, while the man who hates his life in this world will keep it for eternal life. Whoever serves me must follow me; and where I am, my servant also will be. My Father will honour the one who serves me.

'Now my heart is troubled, and what shall I say? "Father, save me from this hour"? No, it was for this very reason I came to this hour. Father, glorify your name!'

Then a voice came from heaven, 'I have glorified it, and will glorify it again.' The crowd that was there and heard it said it had thundered; others said an angel had spoken to him.

Jesus said, 'This voice was for your benefit, not mine. Now is the time for judgment on this world; now the

prince of this world will be driven out. But I, when I am lifted up from the earth, will draw all men to myself.' He said this to show the kind of death he was going to die.

Bible Echoes

In order to fully understand the rich symbols of the snake, the tree and the man which we will be looking at, different people could read out the following verses:
Genesis 3:1
Numbers 21:4–9
John 3:14; 8:28; 12:32–33; 19:28–30
1 Corinthians 15:21–22
Revelation 20:2

Insights

Pontius Pilate was the governor of Judea from AD 26 to 36. It wasn't a very important province so it was ruled by a 'prefect' or 'procurator' who was of lesser status than a Roman senator. The Jews really disliked him because he took things from the treasury in the Temple to pay for a new aqueduct! At the end of his rule he was recalled to Rome because of the violent way in which he crushed a revolt in Samaria.

Pilate was regarded by Jewish historians of the time as being a violent and greedy person but the Jewish religious leaders needed his help in order to kill Jesus. Jewish historians tell us that the religious leaders had lost the right under Roman rule to execute people themselves in about AD 30.

They particularly wanted Jesus to be crucified because this form of death would make Him 'accursed' (Deut. 21:23), and it would signify that the Romans had found

Him guilty of a serious crime. But to John, the author
of John's Gospel, the form of Jesus' death had a deep
prophetic significance. John realised that Jesus would
actually need to be crucified in order to fulfil the
prophecy which said that when He was 'lifted up' He
would draw everyone to Himself (John 12:32).

- What kind of pressures do you think Pilate was under?
- What do you think he really thought about Jesus?

Observations

Three powerful images run through the history of God's
dealings with humanity. A tree, a snake and a Man!

A tree

Our God is a God of promises, and throughout the Bible
we can trace the development of His different covenant
promises with humanity. This started in the Garden of
Eden, when He made a covenant with Adam. This was
a covenant which was entirely dependent on Adam's
obedience regarding the fruit of a special tree in the
Garden. It was there in the Garden of Eden that the devil
used 'a tree' as the means by which humanity was led
into sin and death. For the temptation was to eat from
the tree which made Adam and Eve like God, the fruit of
which led to a knowledge of good and evil and the loss
of innocence (Gen. 3:3–5).

Early Christian teaching by the Church Fathers saw this
tree which led to the Fall as a powerful image picked up
in the life of Jesus when He died on a tree to redeem the
world and to defeat the power of evil.

St Justin the Martyr felt that the tree in the Garden was a
symbol of Christ, and that when the evil one used the tree

to conquer man, this was itself a mystical prophecy of
Christ's future use of the tree to defeat the devil himself.
Justin wrote, 'He who by a tree deceived our forefather
Adam, is by the Cross himself deceived.'

A snake

The other image which runs from the Garden of Eden
right to the end of Scripture is that of a snake. The evil
one was active in the form of a snake in the temptation
of Eve, and was therefore instrumental in the downfall of
humanity and the breaking of the covenant promise.

In Genesis 3:14–15 we read: 'Cursed are you above all the
livestock and all the wild animals ... he will crush your
head, and you will strike his heel.'

Later, in Numbers 21:4–9, we read about a 'plague of
snakes'. The Israelites had been grumbling about Moses
and God and because of their disobedience they are
overwhelmed by a plague of poisonous snakes.

Anyone who has had to deal with just one poisonous
snake will know what a frightening and life-threatening
experience it can be, so it must have been a total
nightmare to face a 'plague' of snakes!

God told Moses to make a bronze snake and lift it up on
a pole. The Bible tells us that anyone who looked at it
was healed! The snake's power was defeated by what was
'lifted up'. It's clear that the author of John's Gospel sees
this incident as a prophetic symbol of what happened
when Jesus was 'lifted up' on a cross.

Some non-biblical records show that victims of crucifixion
at the time of Jesus were nailed through their heel, and
some of the Early Church Fathers saw this as a further
parallel with what happened in the Garden of Eden. They
taught that when someone strikes the head of a snake it
dies, but when someone is bitten on the heel by a snake,

it's not usually fatal, just a temporary wound.
The cross represented only a temporary setback for
Jesus, for three days later He would rise again. But the
cross was the beginning of the end for the power of evil.
Christ's saving work on the cross led to ultimate victory
and the permanent eradication of evil.

A Man

If Adam had kept his part of the covenant promise the
world would have been a very different place, and
rebellion, sin, suffering and death would have been kept
outside the perfection of the created order. But Adam and
Eve broke their promise, and from that instant the world
changed. It was, therefore, a broken promise that broke
the world.

From that instant human beings have lived in a different
world. A world of selfishness, a world in which God has
been rejected, disobeyed and dishonoured. A runaway
world heading towards eternal destruction.

It's a world in which all of the delicate harmonies
of nature are now out of tune, and the innocence of
humanity is stripped away. A world under condemnation
and under the judgment of God.

At the right time, however, God sent His only Son to put
right what had gone wrong, and to redeem the world. If
the first Adam was the source of death and judgment, this
second 'Adam' came as the source of life and salvation.

Talk Time

1. Have you ever held a snake? How did it feel?

_____

_____

_____

2. How would you feel if you faced a 'plague of poisonous snakes'?

_____

_____

_____

3. Why do you think the image of a 'snake' for the power of evil is a strong one?

_____

_____

_____

4. What happens to the 'snake' at the end of time? (See Revelation 20!)

_____

_____

_____

5. Look at the different images of a tree in Genesis, Numbers (a pole in the readings listed under Bible echoes), and in John's description of the crucifixion. What aspect of Christ's work on the cross do they help you understand?

_____

_____

_____

_____

6. Compare what the first Adam and the second Adam did for humanity.

_____

_____

_____

7. There are many ways of understanding the cross
   – what aspects of the crucifixion do these images of
   a snake, a tree and a Man help you in your personal
   understanding?

   _____

   _____

   _____

8. Why is this teaching important for all those who would
   walk the 'way of the cross'?

   _____

   _____

   _____

Response

The way of the cross is a journey which can only be
made in the power of Jesus Christ. A core part of Christian
teaching is that the cross was the battleground between
the cosmic forces of good and evil. Traditional Christian
theology teaches that humanity has been held under the
dominion of the hostile power of evil ever since Adam
and Eve disobeyed God in the Garden of Eden.

A friend of mine once attended a wrestling match in
which a 'caped crusader' was fighting a rather weak-
looking figure who seemed destined to lose from the
very start of the bout. As the match continued, the 'caped
crusader' became more and more aggressive, throwing
his opponent around the ring with complete abandon.
The fight got progressively out of control, until the caped
crusader flung his opponent out of the ring – and when
the referee protested he threw him out of the ring, too!

Just then, as the 'victor' pranced about the ring proclaiming himself the 'champion', the spotlight slowly swung round to the entrance to the hall. There, standing in the doorway, was the famous wrestler 'Big Daddy'. Slowly and confidently he strode down the aisle, hauled himself into the ring, and threw the self-proclaimed 'champion' out of the ring. He then leant over the ropes and pulled the referee and the 'weaker' wrestler back into the ring. He reached out his hands and lifted the arms of the 'defeated' wrestler high. He who had seemingly been defeated was now the winner.

My friend told me that here, in a wrestling ring, he saw a parable of the defeat of Satan and the ultimate victory of One who the crowd thought was powerless and defeated. This is the paradox of the cross. Just when Jesus looked as though He was humiliated and defeated, His Father was beginning to usher in the greatest victory of all.

When we walk the way of the cross we live in the strength of Christ to help us overcome evil today. We also live in the knowledge that His ultimate victory is fast approaching.

- List the different *human* powers and authorities which were ranged against Jesus on His way to the cross.
- How do you believe that the *cosmic* power of evil was at work as well?

Closing Prayers

The Church Father Gregory wrote: 'Just as death was transmitted to all men by a single act, so too, by the action of one Man the principle of resurrection is extended to all humanity.'

At the end of the second century, the great theologian Irenaeus described how the new Adam brings the whole human race into Himself. Of all the Early Church Fathers he expresses most powerfully the concept of Jesus becoming human in order to redeem us. These words of Irenaeus could be read as a meditation over music ...

He was invisible and became visible;
Incomprehensible and became comprehensible;
Incapable of suffering and became subject to suffering;
The Word and became a man;
Recapitulating all things in himself ...
And thus he came even to death,
That he might be the first-born among the dead;
Having pre-eminence in all things;
The prince of life;
The first of all and the one who goes before all ...

- If Jesus defeated evil on the cross, why is there still evil in the world today?
- If we really believe that Jesus has overcome evil, how does this affect our lives today?
- What will heaven be like, when there is no more evil?

the way of
commitment

Key Character: Peter
Keynote Symbol: Bread
Key Challenge: To obey the call of Christ

Conversation Starter

Ask everyone to bring with them a different kind of bread. See who can bring the most original and tasty sample. Someone might like to bake some for the group. (It would probably be wise to have some drinks on hand.)

Try to get as many of the following as possible, cut them up into pieces, get people to sample a mouthful and guess which kind of bread they're tasting. Baguettes, rye bread, split tin, wholemeal tin, plain soda bread, fruit soda bread, sour dough, campaillou, white bloomer, brioche, chollah, seed bread, pitta bread, bagels, bread rolls, scones, rye, croissant, ciabatta, naan, rosemary stick.

- Which is your favourite bread and why?
- Have you ever made bread? How did it work out?
- What does stale bread taste like?

Prayer Time

Display the different kinds of bread on a large plate. Have an open time of prayer thanking God for both the earthly and spiritual food He provides for us.

This poem could then be read as a meditation, possibly over music.

> In a village a boy stood watching
> A baker baking bread
> He watched the kneading of the dough
> And the shaping into loaves
> He felt the heat of the oven's fire
> He smelt that baking smell
> And when they asked him what he'd do
> I'll feed them bread, he said.

A man stood and watched crowds walk away
Taking in lessons learned
His friends gathered left over food
From a meal they all had shared
And twelve baskets full of barley loaves
Was what there was to spare
For when they'd asked him what he'd do
I'll feed them bread, he said.

When the people asked him for a sign
Food sent down from heaven
The truth is I'm the bread
And although you don't believe
If it's life that you are seeking, then
Of me you'll have to eat
I am the bread the Father sent
I'll feed you bread, he said.

This can't be true, in anger they cried
How can we eat your flesh?
Unless you do, he told them all
And also drink of my blood
Then within you there cannot be life.
I give that the world might live
And when you ask me who I am
I'll feed you bread, he said.

And at a table sat the man with
A number of his friends
Taking a loaf, breaking it said
This is my body broken
And the wine in this cup is my blood
Poured out in forgiveness
Eat, drink, so you'll never forget
I'm feeding you bread, he said.

As night fell on the Emmaus road
We ate with a stranger

Who'd shared with us from scripture
And then taken up a loaf
I recognized him as he blessed it
And breaking it, shared it
His body that's broken for me
I'm feeding you bread, he said,
I'm feeding you bread, he said.

by Steven Deal, from 'Breaking Bread'

- Why do you think Jesus used bread as such an important symbol?
- When Jesus fed the 5,000 some of them followed Him around the lake. Why? What were they looking for?
- What kind of bread did Jesus offer them?

Focus

We read in John 21 how the Risen Jesus comes to His disciples at a point of failure. They've been up all night, but caught nothing. He comes as Lord, to demonstrate His power as He provides a multitude of fish. He comes as a servant, to offer them breakfast. He comes as a friend, to share fellowship with them.

When the Risen Jesus broke the bread by the Sea of Galilee it must have been a poignant reminder of the time when He broke the bread for the feeding of the 5,000. The fish which He cooked and broke for them was *opsarion*, dried fish – the very kind that He had used for feeding the 5,000, a poignant reminder of the scene they had also witnessed at Tiberias.

Throughout this encounter with the Risen Jesus the disciples are silent, probably completely overawed by His appearance. It would seem that they fully recognised Him in the breaking of the bread.

As He broke the bread their minds must have gone back to the time when, more recently, He had broken the bread at the Last Supper. Although the meal on the beach was not the Eucharist, it was about the disciples having fellowship with their risen Lord.

- Have there been any occasions when celebrating the Last Supper has been especially meaningful for you?

Bible Reading

John 21:12-19
Jesus Reinstates Peter

Jesus said to them, 'Come and have breakfast.' None of the disciples dared ask him, 'Who are you?' They knew it was the Lord. Jesus came, took the bread and gave it to them, and did the same with the fish. This was now the third time Jesus appeared to his disciples after he was raised from the dead.

When they had finished eating, Jesus said to Simon Peter, 'Simon son of John, do you truly love me more than these?'

'Yes, Lord,' he said, 'you know that I love you.'

Jesus said, 'Feed my lambs.'

Again Jesus said, 'Simon son of John, do you truly love me?'

He answered, 'Yes, Lord, you know that I love you.'

Jesus said, 'Take care of my sheep.'

The third time he said to him, 'Simon son of John, do you love me?'

Peter was hurt because Jesus asked him the third time, 'Do you love me?' He said, 'Lord, you know all things; you know that I love you.'

Jesus said, 'Feed my sheep. I tell you the truth, when you were younger you dressed yourself and went where you wanted; but when you are old you will stretch out your hands, and someone else will dress you and lead

you where you do not want to go.' Jesus said this to indicate the kind of death by which Peter would glorify God. Then he said to him, 'Follow me!'

- Why do you think these disciples had gone back to Galilee – out of rebellion or obedience?
- How do you think the disciples felt after their night of fishing?
- How do you think Peter felt when Jesus asked him these questions?

Bible Echoes

Look up the following verses:
Genesis 49:24
Psalm 80:1
Isaiah 40:11
2 Samuel 5:2
Jeremiah 23:4
Ezekiel 34
John 10:1–18
Acts 20:28
1 Peter 2:25; 5:1–4

- How did the people of Israel see the image of sheep and shepherds?
- How did Jesus apply it to His own ministry?
- How did Peter become a shepherd?
- What kind of shepherd do you think Peter was?

Insights

When Peter met Jesus on the beach their conversation was both moving and dramatic. Scholars have discussed at great length the words and phrases used, and it's clear that whatever interpretation is placed on the words there is great spiritual power here.

Jesus asks Peter if he loves Him more than 'these'. Scholars debate as to whether 'these' refers to the boat and the nets. Perhaps Jesus is asking Peter if his new calling to be an evangelist and church leader isn't more urgent and important than his previous job as a fisherman.

Others think that Jesus may be referring to Peter's relationship with the other disciples, as compared to Him. In other words, does he love Jesus more than he loves these other disciples? Is his relationship with the Risen Christ more important to him than his human friendships?

The most poignant meaning, however, is different. Does Peter love Jesus more than the other disciples do? After all his proud promises that he will never forsake his Lord – no matter what the other disciples would do – have been broken. Jesus is pinpointing his pride. Does he *really* love Him more than these other disciples?

This conversation challenges us to think through our love for Jesus. Is it the greatest love of all, and is it at the very core of our being? True Christian commitment must be driven by such a love, or it is nothing more than a duty-driven set of obligations!

Observations

One of the interesting observations which Bible scholars make about this passage involves the words used for 'love'. In the first two questions Jesus uses a word which can be interpreted in some circumstances as a 'false love' (*agapao*) or a 'compromised love'. Peter replies with a

word for love that is different, but implies strong human love (*phileo*). On the third occasion Jesus changes His word to the same word Peter has used.

Just as Peter denied his Lord three times, so he is asked to affirm his love for Jesus three times. There is great hope and strength here for anyone who ever feels that they have broken a commitment to Jesus, or that they need to start again in their life of discipleship.

The meaning of the words 'sheep' and 'lambs' is also much debated. Most importantly, however, is the commission given by Jesus to care for others. A commission which Peter went forward to demonstrate with great power in the Acts of the Apostles.

This conversation reminds us of our great need to be committed to Jesus, to love Him, and to serve Him by caring for others through His love.

Talk Time

Look up Exodus 16.

The people of Israel called the bread manna. It was white like coriander seed and tasted like wafers made with honey. Moses said, 'This is what the LORD has commanded: "Take an omer of manna and keep it for the generations to come, so they can see the bread I gave you to eat in the desert when I brought you out of Egypt."' (vv.31–32)

1. How were the people fed?

2. What do you think the bread tasted like?

3. Why couldn't they keep it?

4. What was the symbolism of the need to gather it daily?

5. How does the symbolism of this story enrich our understanding of the feeding of the 5,000, the Last Supper and the meal on the beach?

6. When we refer to Jesus as the 'Bread of Life' what do we mean?

7. How is Jesus relevant to your everyday life?

_____

_____

_____

Response

Peter was determined to commit to Jesus. In the different Gospels we read slightly different promises which he made to Jesus. He broke his promises and failed in his commitment, but after the Resurrection he was reconciled to Jesus again. If we have broken commitments made to Jesus across the years we can take heart from Peter's experience of fresh grace and a new beginning.

Read the different promises he made.

'But he replied, "Lord, I am ready to go with you to prison and to death"' (Luke 22:33).
'But Peter declared, "Even if I have to die with you, I will never disown you." And all the other disciples said the same' (Matt. 26:35).
'Peter asked, "Lord, why can't I follow you now? I will lay down my life for you"' (John 13:37).

- What did Peter offer to do?
- What did he actually do? Why?
- How do you think he felt when he failed?
- Are you ready to make a promise to Jesus; if so, what would be your commitment?
- What happens if we make a commitment but fail?

Closing Devotions

We close by using the words of the hymn-writer Horatius Bonar (1808–1889) as a prayer.

Upon a Life I have not lived,
Upon a Death I did not die,
Another's Life, Another's Death;
I stake my whole eternity.

Not on the tears which I have shed;
Not on the sorrows I have known;
Another's tears; Another's griefs;
On them I rest, on them alone.

Jesus, O Son of God, I build
On what Thy cross has done for me;
There both my death and life I read;
My guilt, my pardon there I see.

Lord, I believe; O deal with me
As one who has Thy Word believed!
I take the gift, Lord, look on me
As one who has Thy gift received.

The Early Church Father, Augustine, once wrote:

Grant me to know thee.
Grant me, even me, my dearest Lord, to know thee, and
love thee, and rejoice in thee. And if I cannot do these
perfectly in this life, let me at least advance to higher
degrees every day, til I can come to do them in perfection. Let the knowledge of thee increase in me here,
that it may be full hereafter. Let the love of thee grow
every day more and more here, that it may be perfect
hereafter; that my joy may be great in itself, and full in
thee. I know, O God, that thou art a God of truth. Oh,
make good thy gracious promises to me, that my joy
may be full. Amen.

Close the final devotional time with a Holy Communion
or Eucharist, and an open time of 'commitment' prayers
for the future.

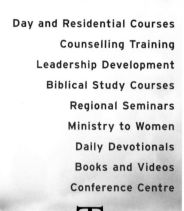

Day and Residential Courses

Counselling Training

Leadership Development

Biblical Study Courses

Regional Seminars

Ministry to Women

Daily Devotionals

Books and Videos

Conference Centre

Trusted all Over the World

CWR HAS GAINED A WORLDWIDE reputation as a centre of excellence for Bible-based training and resources. From our headquarters at Waverley Abbey House, Farnham, England, we have been serving God's people for 40 years with a vision to help apply God's Word to everyday life and relationships. The daily devotional *Every Day with Jesus* is read by nearly a million readers an issue in more than 150 countries, and our unique courses in biblical studies and pastoral care are respected all over the world. Waverley Abbey House provides a conference centre in a tranquil setting.

For free brochures on our seminars and courses, conference facilities, or a catalogue of CWR resources, please contact us at the following address. **CWR, Waverley Abbey House, Waverley Lane, Farnham, Surrey GU9 8EP, UK**

Telephone: **+44 (0)1252 784700**
Email: **mail@cwr.org.uk**
Website: **www.cwr.org.uk**

CWR CRUSADE FOR WORLD REVIVAL
Applying God's Word to everyday life and relationships